VIA Folios 122

DIAGNOSTICS

POETICS OF TIME

DIAGNOSTICS
POETICS OF TIME

Joseph A. Amato

BORDIGHERA PRESS

Library of Congress Control Number: 2017941318

Cover Art:
Felice Amato, *Divination*, 2016
mixed media on canvas

Printed in the United States.

Published by
BORDIGHERA PRESS
John D. Calandra Italian American Institute
25 West 43rd Street, 17th Floor
New York, NY 10036

VIA FOLIOS 122
ISBN 978-1-59954-117-4

Gods have immediate knowledge of invisible and
mortal things, but men must proceed by clues.

Umberto Eco, *Semiotics and the Philosophy of Language*

For one I give myself up to the abandonment of the
time and place.

Herman Melville, *Moby Dick*

Now is the time to ask your destinies!

Virgil, *The Aeneid*

Table of Contents

Preface and Acknowledgments

Diagnostics, Poetics of Time is a collection of poems on our attempts to read, or by diagnostics' Greek roots, to distinguish and discern, our place and condition in time. And it is the root sense of poesis that explains the subtitle *Poetics of Time*: to make or bring forth meanings of lives lived out in times, constant and many.

The personal tributaries of my immediate and long-term interest in history, temporality, and mortality are found in the concluding essay of this work, Part V, "Now is Rife with Next." Beyond this, I can only hope that my poems speak for themselves and convey fresh insights that offer companionship of experience and feeling.

This work strengthened and established my sense of gratitude. As always and in the case of this work in particular, I am indebted to my wife, Catherine, and her buoyant spirit, who in her own words keeps on plugin'. She is Christian pilgrim and coal miner's granddaughter.

Thanks also go to our children, my loyal sister-in-law, Jean Davenport, abiding friends, researchers, and Mayo doctors, especially hematologist Dr. Erin Schenk and heart surgeon Dr. Lyle Joyce. In turn, I made good use of Mayo Clinic's libraries and medical resources.

I wish to thank again readers Dana Yost and Michael Palma, and I am especially indebted to trusted reader and copyeditor Suzanne Noguere, who with great talent helped bring form out of flux.

To my daughter Felice Amato, I give both thanks and admiration for the cover art for this work. Thanks to friend and master of "shaky art," Morris Gillett, for the drawing of a humming bird, on page 92.

And once again I express my deep gratitude to Bordighera Press, its director Anthony Tamburri, and editor Nick Grosso for welcoming and producing the book you have before you.

Prelude

Names, The Communion of Being

When I say your name, Cathy,
I take you in communion,
And so you take me in
By my name.

You and I,
Identities whispered and said,
None more certain.
We baptize each other
By saying our names
As once we married each other
With them.
Now names marry us
To the fullness of the days
And carry us out of dark places
As across the years,
Love and fidelity certain,
Trust unbroken.

I. CERTITUDES

Cottonwood Seed

Come mid May,
Along rain-risen rivers
Cottonwood seed
Glides, floats, and hovers.

The revelation
Of a great generosity,
Fluff so gently light,
Soft and white,
So alive to the least breeze,
The epiphany
Of falling seed
Drops a silk canopy
Over spring's wedding.

A Dead Cardinal

Along a small winding path
Above the marsh,
Below a high rise,
I walk mulling on the proposition:
Attention makes true;
It fills the cellars of memory,
Contours imagination,
Focuses the will,
And offers urgency and weight to every judgment.

And then,
There at my feet,
On the cracked black asphalt
Lies a dead cardinal,
Burnished, tan, grey, and orange,
Fixed, frozen,
As if alive forever in its death.

I pick it up by its wing—
No wound or bruise
On body, head, or beak—
And set it on a bank of glacial stones,
Its catafalque.

With it,
All of nature lies in state
In open air,
Awaiting a scavenging fox
Or the wakening of the bird lord.

I walk away attentive.
How random the death of beauty,
And how random the beauty of death.

A Moment, A Morning

A memory still vivid
From my boyhood river days:

Once, as a boy,
I waded the banks of a river
With a new thirty-five-pound reflex bow and arrow
I bought from Epps,
A popular army surplus store
On Gratiot Avenue
Between Seven and Eight Mile roads.

In the shallows I spied a northern pike
That glittered as it lingered in the shadows.
Its tail swayed
Slowly,
A pendulum of river time.
As I pulled, I aimed and trembled —
Then in an instant — released
And missed.
Retrieving my arrow,
I went further down river
Towards the weeds and pools
In which big carp
Splashed and spawned
And then swiftly swam away
From another missed shot
In a wiggle and curve of "S's"
And a screen of rising mud.

Lake Breeze

The screen door slams shut,
And suddenly the breeze comes up.
Ripples in a rush
Lap noisily against the sides of the cabin's two canoes,
Which, tethered by front and back ropes,
Swing to and fro,
Nudging and nestling against the dock —
Overgrown aluminum puppies
Futilely searching a milking tit.

Along the shore,
Where eagles and osprey soar,
The breeze sings
Through stands of tall red and white pines.

Again the screen door slams shut,
Crystals of morning dew vanish
As the children rush noisily
Toward the dock,
Now and for the first time ever
Onto the bright blue stage
Of a day's watery play
On this small humble lake.

At Aunt Mabel's Cottage

Past Mt. Clemens, Selfridge Field Air Base,
And only several houses from the mouth
Of the Clinton River on Conger Bay of Lake St. Clair,
Stood Aunt Mabel's small, white three-room cottage.
With sea-blue shutters it invited you off the short
Two-lane gravel road into an ample yard,
A chore to mow with a rusty hand-pushed mower.

Contrastingly, the small front yard
Gently declined toward the water,
Which each year crept further onto the land,
Lapping over and covering the planking of Mabel's dock,
Whose moss surface made it grease slick.
In an instant my feet came out from under me
And I remember going down, coming up, and going down,
Until a hand reached out and grasped me.

Following the advancing water, cattails and lily pads
Steadily, stealthily, reclaimed the shallows.
Annual dredging of canals alone permitted escape.
Along their deepest channels,
Sunken logs and abandoned fishing houses accumulated.
On sunny days snapping turtles appeared
And with a slide and plop disappeared.
Once I rowed my grandmother out to first open waters,
For an afternoon's fishing, which she,
A river-raised girl, cherished.
Our reward: a harvest of pan fish
For an evening feast,
Prefaced, as all such meals were, by the caution:
Watch out for fish bones.

The great open bay waters beyond
Held greater risks for boaters,
Should they venture out
On those days when great red rings were laid as targets
For planes to practice bombing runs,
Dropping sandbags.

Next to Mabel's cabin was an empty weed-filled lot
And Krausie's big story-high dock
Where we dived and swam
And came to shore
With black blood suckers on us,
Two, three, four, and even more.

Inside Mabel's cabin
Hung spirals of yellow-tan flypaper.
I counted the mystery and number of stuck flies.
Once buzzing,
Lively, all about,
Then stuck,
Soon and forever dead.
For a moment,
I pitied them.
Under Mabel's side porch,
The only way in and out,
A woodpile,
Out of which snakes constantly poked their heads,
Flashed and flicked their probing forked tongues,
Taking in the world,
Of which, come night,
They would take hold.

Once my grandfather drove me home
In his '37 Chevy convertible,
Forest green,
With a rumble seat.
The fog had settled so deep on Conger Bay
That his yellow fog lights

Barely showed the way
Along to the gravel road
To the asphalt
And the fenced and guarded entrance of the airbase,
Before whose distant hangars
One or two ominous warplanes perched.

Burr Oak

The burr oak is the Shakespeare of trees.
With their thick, reaching, gnarled limbs,
Broken and irregular canopies,
They sketch the skies,
With their tortured fate.
Guarding the prairie's rim
Against grass fires,
They long ago
Kidnapped my eyes
With their crooked defiance
Of drooping pine and weeping willow,
Every tree of straight limbs
And predictable symmetry.

The Great Live Oak

With sturdy long limbs and twisted branches
beckoning with the crooked twig fingers of a witch,
the live oak forms an immense umbrella in
these scorching summer sunshine days.
Its great
girth is
a shaft
linking
earth
to sky,
planting
me too
on this
trembling
ground
amid the undulating horizon-chasing hills and passing clouds.

Patriarch Red Oaks

Red oaks quarrel with space.
Bent and sculpted, they argue against symmetry,
Their thick, crooked branches
Twisted left and right,
Elbow up and down.
Ornery,
Obstinate,
Strong-willed,
Of earth's tangled roots,
They believe in and argue for the sky.
They carry green's grace high.

Wake Up, Spring Will Come

The land is bedded in snow,
Capped in mist,
White, white, all around,
All quiet, still in space and time.
No breath giving life to the air,
No prophecy declared
By barren trunk and stark branch,
Whispered in huddles of dark green pine.
Save yourself from the surrounding nothing.
Remember light-blaring sun
And bird-noisy spring,
Water's fresh, alerting run
And the colorful blooming
Of what was once dead.

Time Dances Us Silly

Awake,
Alive by glance,
We arrive
At the dance.

Our partner,
Club- and wing-footed Time,
Does not dance
To any long predictable beat.

Braiding
Each dance to speedy fortune
And slow fate,
He steps and spins us
To the instant,
The trudge of the seasons,
The twisting circles
Of beginnings and ends.

Of subtle, graceful steps,
And clumsy boot-clops,
He puts us out of time
As we try to step
To birth and death,
Love and war.
So our partner Time
Dances us silly.
Our senses do not make sense.
His shuddering steps
Twirl us inward.
There, momentarily off the floor,
What philosophers call a second reality

Of thought, mind, self, and soul,
Where foot rarely touches ground,
We augur and pray
That somehow,
Once or next,
We dance in tune.

Twos

Thick-thighed dwarfs
With a waddling stride,

Dragonflies darting
Across a fresh spring swamp —

Oppositions and juxtapositions
Grab our attention,

Teaching us nothing
But about us.

Near and Far

Boyhood was all about luck,
The magic phrase that got me a single,
The secret wish that delivered a gift,
The red stone I rubbed,
The checkered shirt I wore inside out,
The number seven,
Which my father and uncles got on their knees
To chant, shake, and blow on the dice,
And then roll hard against the freshly painted scrub board.

Childhood for me was about what I always desired
And found only once in a while.
It was not about fate,
The sea to be crossed,
The mother dead and vanished in a day,
The malady for which there is no therapy.
Death was always in never time,
It belonged to someone else
Or times unimaginably far.

Now in old age,
I sit at the banks of a great and gathering river,
Fishing cherished memory,
Bathing in days numbered certain
And destined to end
Around the next great bend.

Poets

Like physicists in search of smallest particles
Astronomers questing evidence of a black hole,
Geologists tracking the movement of the deepest plates,
Or radiologists scanning the marrow of inner bone,
Poets sound the hollows of the heart
With the weighted line of language.

Writing Bone

Take up the priestly art
And write.
With sharpened bone,
In soft clay,

Write your name,
Be remembered,
Spared time's course
More than an overrun power,
A crumbled tower,
A forgotten ruler.
Be a lasting word,
Young, hopeful writer.

II. UNCERTAINTIES

River Eggs
Fourth of July, 2014

One May,
In the cold and coursing Huron River,
As young scouts we swam
Out from the old dock,
Through sheets of floating frog eggs.
Toward the far shore
We stood waist-deep in the water,
Balancing
On a submerged, slippery tree trunk.

Suddenly, a big black water snake surfaced
And opened its mouth
As if to gulp down and swallow the sun.

It vanished below
With the approach of our worst swimmer,
Who swam with head down,
Pawing air and water,
Propelled by frantic arms
And an erratic kick.

He never saw the snake
Anymore than he saw the car
He hit head on
Six years later
On the way downtown
To our high school graduation dance.
His pregnant girlfriend survived,
Her five-month-old fetus
Did not.

Yesterday,
July Third,
Fifty-eight years
After those deaths,
News again.
As it comes everyday,
It features precarious us
On the way down river:
While the stock market reached a new high,
Over 17,000,
Ebola spread in Africa.
Young men and women killed young men and women in
Syria.
And blood again rained in the Ukraine.

Scientists fudged their stem-cell science.
Children, without mothers and fathers, came
Across southern borders in droves,
Thousands upon thousands.
A big sea surge announced a pending storm
On the outer banks.

Closer to home,
In nearby Granite Falls, Minnesota,
A seventeen-year-old boy was sentenced
To life in prison:
He had instigated the robbery
Of his grandmother,
Possibly precipitating her death
In the course of the crime.
Elsewhere in Minnesota,
A father crashed his car
And then fled,
Leaving his injured son and daughter
Calling for help.
One of them had a broken neck.

So time,
So history,
So abundant and superfluous life,
Eggs on a spring river float downstream,
And life encapsulated in embryo
In cars and the cockpits of fighter planes
Moves joylessly, mindlessly, and cruelly.

With knife, gun, and rocket
We cut a tangle of knots.
We tread senseless chaos
With cunning, guile, and beauty.
We shape our arts,
Ply our crafts
To float creation anew,
Spring frog eggs
Moving downstream.

The Devil in the Cap

Andreas Lubitz, co-pilot of Germanwings 9525, March 24, 2015

1: Prelude

Though you tie strings
To your puppets,
Stories elude manipulation.
Evil has no telling, madness no measure.
There is no string through a heartless mind.

Around the rim of his smoldering self
Out of which lava runs and sulfur leaks —
Up from the black pit of himself
Swallowing fumes and fuming —
In the swirl of his thoughts
Circling inward ever faster,
A vortex now vertigo —
Only the story calls out
Beyond the whirlpool:
I will make my will yours —
The world's;
Even God and child
Will sing
In my chorus.

On a table, the two-month diary
Recording his descent
Into inescapable
Depression,
Merciless
Depravity.

2: The Act

On his head the co-pilot puts
A yellow-goggled helmet
Of jumping lice and white maggots.
It becomes his buzzing, putrid crown
Of angry bees, zigzagging bats,
And hunting night-flying owls.

Inside his head
Neurons are stitched together,
Axons and dendrites stretched
Like black spider's white silk.
He is wired with hate
And aims to make his fiery crash
Global theater.

He locks the captain out
And flies his dark design.

Before him the mountain,
Inverse of his cratered self.
As his target approaches,
He descends swiftly to meet it,
Fleeing the last pull
Of grace, and memory
Of his mother's buoyant face.

Anxious, gleeful,
All that remains:
Clinching the ecstasy
Of a spiteful end.

No call, no plea
Reaches him.
Relentless, disdaining all voices
And banging
At the cabin's door,
He descends into the final shadow

Of Alpine mountain and ravine.

Singing, humming, to himself,
He announces to all:
I, the captain of spite,
Fly the downward course
Of black ire.

Uncle Sam's Fly

Uncle Sam stood in front of a window
That looked out on a small yard,
A sliver of a garden,
And the garage
That once housed the horse and cart
From which my father,
When only a boy of seven,
Sold fruit
To nearby factory workers.

Sam,
Who threw the ball hard
In our games of catch
And had survived the Italian campaign
And brought back a German Luger, flag, and helmet,
Swatted a fly
That lit on the oilcloth table cover
Among the black seeds
Of a freshly sliced
Georgia watermelon.

Out of the blue,
Sam declared that a house fly
Lives only a twenty-four-hour life.
My Uncle Jimmy,
Whose tour of infantry duty
Went from Sicily up the boot of Italy
Then over to Normandy
And finally into Germany
And tallied fourteen killed enemies,
Disagreed with Sam.
My dad did too.

But Sam stood his ground
In what proved an amicable go-around.

Sam died two years
After that kitchen debate
Over the life of a fly.
Stomach cancer
Took him prisoner
For eighteen months,
Reducing a two-hundred-pound man
To a hundred,
Refusing even a Christmas truce.

Revenant

How is it that today love arose within me
Seventy years after we played catch?
We drank in each other's smile —
Throw and catch.

Seventy years since wasting stomach cancer
Nibbled you down,
Soldier of the Great War.
You became a skeleton of yourself
As you melted to a dark, bony puddle of a being,
Jaundiced in your bed,
Your eyes bulging wildly.

I hid in the kitchen,
Afraid to drink from any glass
That you might have sipped.
You have left the circle of even imaginative embrace.

Again, now, a whole lifetime later,
When I am ready to take to my bed,
I hold your hand,
Drink from your generous face.
You and I
And veteran uncles Jimmy and Bill,
Dance, one foot up and the other solidly down.
We prance a watery circle
Through the prism of youth
Mine yet yours,
Buoyant — bouncing
Our joyous line
Leading from here to there,
To God,
Beyond time.

The Reason Why

Because I know my skin
I do not go to war easily.
Skin soft,
Quick to hurt and pain,
Hand of love's touch,
Alive but once
To a mother's caress
And father's crafting hands.

Incarnate,
Creation of divine handiwork,
Participant in its forms
Blessed at times with such living hopes,
Cherishing love, forgiveness, and mercy,
Dare we of sensual flesh go to war easily,
Take up the day's harsh enthusiasms,
Surrender to the son's heroic ways
And father's rock-certain will
And age-conceded command
To kill?

O God, Where Is My Brother?
Jeremy Bush, February 28, 2013, Seffner, Florida

I threw open the door
Of my brother's room—
No more, empty, a vacuum.
Only the corner
Of his bed protruded
From the earth,
From the hole in the earth.
I jumped in
And dug by hand,
Then shoveled
After his body.

The earth has swallowed
The brother
From whom I was never apart.
Sorrowfully, I continue to round the rim
Of that night's sinkhole,
Suspended
In his continuing fall.

Though days pass,
I still trudge in mind
Through limestone caverns
Towards a primordial sea,
The bottom of oblivion.

With head bent down,
I kick and shuffle
Along the path
Of an old truth:
That the soul is the image

Of the body,
And the body resides, dwells
In flesh
Pressed close,
Fused
One
In this life.

Even from the tip of my toes
I can't peer beyond
The chasm of his fall
And the abyss
Of my sunken heart.

The black and white maypole
Of memory,
Born of the same bed and table,
Boiling pot
And ember-filled hearth,
Has been pulled —
Wound, rusty, barbwire tight.

And so
I circle this crater,
This empty Jericho,
Lamenting, supplicating:
"O God,
Where is my brother?"

Born to a Sawdust Ring

To my birth
In the back alley of a carnival
Came a blind astrologer
Who muttered doubts
About stars, stories, and metaphors.

To my fifth birthday
Came a defrocked priest,
A clown
Who refused to wear makeup
And turned crooked somersaults and awkward cartwheels.

Behind them
Came an old flabby elephant
Whose swinging trunk
Was a metronome of my life
On this circling sawdust trail.

A Poetic Encyclopedia of Agnosia

We cannot walk the length of night,
Inventory the zoo of human ignorance.
Stupidity, craziness, foolish risk-taking, Alzheimer's—
We are without a science of ignorance,
An "encyclopedia of agnosia."

There are those whose experience is not their own:
Who do not know that their sexual organs are their own,
Who cannot identify forms and faces,
Make sense of words and sounds,
Establish sequences to mind or life.

There are those without memory or sympathy,
Those who disinterestedly step over their hard black turds
And cannot dam their slobbering drool,
While others flee for the future on magic boards
And the coming and going of zodiac signs.
Yet others have their pleasure in not knowing what is next:
The suspense and surprise
Of the roll of dice, the flip of a coin, the deal and show of
cards.

Then there is me:
When not in the guidance of television and newspaper,
I shape my diagnostics by the dead-reckoning,
The current, slosh, and surge
Of daily appearances and interpreting coincidence.
In time's pinch, I read the changing ideograms of flocks of
passing geese,
And ride two-headed sea turtles deep down into ocean crypts,
And know earth and light by the path of rising bubbles,
And navigate the beyond by prayer.

Apropos of Seating

Mind is about
What is sitting next to what,
Who to whom,
And what will they do next,
All this intuitively obvious or subtly ambiguous,
Hypothetical, conjectural, or debatable
And includes questions whether, after all,
There even is a chair,
And appropriate propositions
About proper posture.
Uncertainties abound,
And so we philosophers suffer
And delight in turning around
And around.

Mindfulness

How sly the mind,
How cunning our ways:
With a turn of phrase,
With gesturing words for sword,
Lips our hilt,
The thrust and parry of our blade
Didactic pronunciation,
Keen elucidation,
And feinting digression,
We would stand triumphant
Over what we say.

But the old trickster
Is not tricked:
Conscience,
Out the blue,
Will self-accuse.

Then memory, ever ready,
Takes the stand against us,
Testifying to clandestine meetings
Where the heart kept silent.

Sorting Out

1

We take ourselves,
Believe ourselves,
To be — somewhere, somehow —
One with ourselves,
Though we count ourselves many
With every glance
Seeing and being seen.

Surely, we postulate ourselves
One and whole
In our mother's womb.
We were one and whole —
Our youthful catechism made us so —
By virtue of an everlasting soul
And His son's passionate and personal embrace
Of this divine errant race.

And beyond all reason,
We take our identity,
If secured by the whisper of our name alone,
To have an everlasting continuity.
(And our play of the game
Might win us captivating fame.)
And then, if deeper truth were told,
There is our heart's sincerity
And its promised lifelong fidelity.

2

But integrity and unity,
However much we hope,

Do not match our bent paths
Or square with our crooked lot.
Like Hamlet
On the foggy rampart
Along a graveyard path,
We ever return to the crossroad:
To be or not to be.

Like the widow
Evacuating her lifelong home,
I seek to braid and unbraid
Memories — photos and things,
Gifts and keepsakes.
I live today
In the congestion
Of yesterday's giving and taking.

Son or daughter?
Before the donation bin
Of the thrift store
I come unraveled
Amid the emotional commotion
Of things given and received.

3

Adrift in time,
I seek the string of yesteryears
Through the maze
Of current days.

The teeter-totter goes up and down,
The merry-go-round goes round and round,
And the tick and tock of life's clock:
This then that! That then this!
The sounding pendulum
Of my divided and vacillating self.

4

On the uncombed beach
Of mind
Things are thrown up as 1 and 2.
With each discrete breath,
I discern mortality.
And then, I count a 1 plus 2 equals 3,
Forming a momentary trinity,
An ephemeral unity.

Counting and calibrating,
With a straw between my teeth,
Square dancing I go.
"All hands around."
And then a grand "How do you do?"

First bow to neighbor on your left,
Then your right,
Then do-si-do your partner.
Take your partner's hands,
Swing her good,
And promenade.

Now it is "Grand Right and Left,"
All men circle right and women left.
When you get back home and meet your lovely partner
Swing her good again.

5

I am a kingdom of symptoms
From skin to innards,
From aching back to
Shortness of breath,
All the signs of coming death.
Diagnosis and prognosis
Afford no oasis.

A rusty hinge swings
Out into the gravel alley
Where rats run furtively
And sparrows flock
Around the garbage stand
And stray hollyhocks.

The priest presages,
Someone reads the sky,
Another feels my face
To read my fortune.
One says I am surely blessed,
And another taps on my head
And judges me an empty casket
Soon to be filled with death.

6

All I have is that old Mediterranean tale
Of Athenian craftsman Daedalus and son Icarus
Who went to Crete
And built the sinful frame
For the island's royal queen Pasiphaë's sin
And Minos's and the island's everlasting shame.

And though with freshly-crafted waxen wings
Daedalus and Icarus escaped the labyrinth
And its bestiality-bred Minotaur,
Brazen Icarus flew up too close to the sun
And with melted wings
Plunged steep and deep
Into the black sea.

Father and son,
Ever an unequal symmetry,
Are not made to conspire,
To share beds of sweat
And dreams.
A mother and women

Were created to keep son and father apart.
They are not meant to be nose to nose,
To aspire and conspire together.

The son said:

> *I loved my father,*
> *I hated my father,*
> *I will do anything I can to please him.*

Each has a fortune and fate
With his own date.

7

But beyond my Mediterranean stories
And Sicilian proverbs,
The blessed among us
Are those whose faith carries them
On a stable, securing course.
Those who are graced to hope
That in the end,
Beyond the testing twos
And the baffling many,
They will see
The blessed epiphany
Of the Trinity,
And living and dead in unity.

Species of Flight

The nest —
Hub and home,
Center of concentric circles
Of eagles' scavenging life,
Where male and female meet and mate.
Twigs and grasses circle and secure
Eggs brooded in the warming feathery down.
As fish bones multiply,
Chicks grow,
Honing talons and beaks
To fly across seasons
In the light of the sun
On updrafts
And across the face
Of the waning moon.

And I, who have slept a life
In modern comfort's bed,
Find no rest,
Having left the nest
Of my mother's lap,
My father's workbench,
In the service of words.
I have taken on their high-flying manifest,
Knowing that language does not fly free
Of doubt's downdrafts
Or truth's hurricanes.

In Time's Rapids

Taken on mortality's stainless-steel barbed hook,
A nylon line that does not break,
I, a fish
In earth's temporal waters,
Echo Christ's words:
"My God!
Why have you forsaken me?"

Such a Big Word

Diagnosis,
Such a big word
For telling me whether I am sick or well,
Whether I will live out the year
Or die tomorrow.
Time ticks.
Life passes.
Pain alerts.
Out of the blue, tests warn.

I walk precariously
Amid mounting symptoms
And medical appointments,
Banging bedpans and carts of tingling glass,
Between fear of diminishing
(An abruptly ending day)

And hope that faith and belief
Prove true
Beyond testing parables
And books of prophecies.

III. DIAGNOSIS

A Fall Rose

Blocks away from where flags flap
And clang on steel poles,
On our dead-end street
A single red rose bobs
In a gentle evening breeze.
A fine fall light fills my eyes
With autumn's auburns
And tries my heart
With night's deepening alert.

Yates Cider Mill

One golden fall day
When the harvest was underway,
Orchards brimmed with fruit
And apples were red, sweet, and ready
As my mother, father, my grandmother Rosalia, and I
Drove north out of Detroit—towards Auburn Hills and Rochester—
To Yates Cider Mill.

Situated on the banks of the Clinton River,
Once known as *Nottwasippee*, Ojibway for Rattlesnake River,
The mill, housed in a red-planked building
On the upper pond's side,
Had stood there
Since the Civil War.

A bag of apples in full color and innocence
Was the edible prize of our trip.
The mill churned for me,
Telling the permanence of youth,
While it turned Rosalia back to another truth
She never failed habitually to repeat:
Her Sicily, too,
Was equally rich in greens, fruits—
And olive trees.

Now, sixty-five years later
On a bright September day,
My wife and I travel east
From southwest Minnesota
Across soon-to-harvest
Withered brown soybean and yellow wrinkled cornfields

Along the green Minnesota River valley,
Fingers of the great Indian uprising,
Past New Ulm and Mankato
To Rochester,
To Mayo,
A world-renowned medical mill,
For a diagnosis,
Prognosis.

Mayo, Our Delos

The black asphalt road
Cuts a swath through the green
Of rolling hills of grain;
And dark rivers
Born of spring's abundant rains
Cut a valley's secret terrain.
Bubbled clouds bounce gently across the horizon
As we pound and thump
Our dumb, recurrent morning way
In our blue Honda
To Mayo,
Our Delos,
Isle of hope,
Sanctuary of best therapy.

On the Way to Mayo

Dark, somber pines
Stand sullen green
On spring grass.
Indifferent to fresh rains,
They crowd close
On this sunless grey day
And overrule the spring.

Dark Pines

Along the side of Highway 52
From Minnetonka to Rochester,
Again today the somber pines

Stand huddled and persistent —
Sentinels of winter's darkest shadows
And Rochester's stark diagnoses.

A Fruit Market Puzzle in the Waiting Room

A breast bubbles up
From a loose blouse.
It sprouts
Fresh and ripe
From a daughter leaning over
To help a frail mother
Complete a farm puzzle.

The puzzle has a big brown barn,
A green garden,
And, on a table,
A cornucopia of vegetables —
Artichokes, asparagus, squash, yellow pears,
Green beans, a pumpkin, and a line of red tomatoes.

Out of words,
We kill time watching
A mother and daughter kill time.
We wait for the red and white cell count
Of hematology,
Hoping in a higher mercy —
A diagnosis predicting
A quick healing.

With the puzzle still undone,
The mother and daughter enter ominous Door Four.
We continue to wait
At the threshold of Door Four.

The nurse summons us
With a smile
And weighs my wife.

The doctor soon will give medicine's accounting,
Reveal the count
Of white and red cells.
A half-century of hard habit and loyal love
Goes uncalculated.

Give Yourself to Medicine

Give yourself to medicine,
Go gentle into that hopeful night.
Be examined,
Roll up your sleeves,
Disrobe,
Be ready for probes and scopes,
For scans,
Bombardments
By particles, subatomic small.
Lie flat and still
In a grey metallic coffin-like cylinder,
Listen to sirens of clanging magnets.
Sail by dissecting poles,
Coasts of blood, bone, and organ.

Take a seat,
Make a fist
For the prick of a vein
Or surrender an arm for transfusion
Of chemicals unknown,
Molecules of recent design.
Your prognosis belongs to labs near and far
For analysis for hours and weeks,
Compounded numbers and graphs.
Until your doctor breaks the news,
There will be more of the same,
Or you are pronounced free and whole—
Welcome to go.

Like the child who skips home from confession,
Absolved of first mortal sin,
You walk, if you still can,

Briskly, lightly, to the parking lot,
Ready to drive out of tightening circles
Of diagnosis, therapy, and again diagnosis,
Among shifting shadows of prognosis.

Again travel free from the kingdom of symptoms,
From the recurrence of omens,
To a place not clouded by worry, anxiety, and augury,
Ambiguity and equivocation,
To a distinct landscape of fresh running waters,
High grassy knolls,
In light winds,
Under open skies
With eyes enraptured,
Riding the tips of balancing and gliding wings.

Of Marrow and Morrow

It lurks below the hospital's finest scans
And sensitive tests:
Invisible, amorphous, the black monster,
The shark cancer
Breeds deep in the body's ocean of cells,
In the marrow of sand and shell.
It grows cutting fins,
Rows of great sharp teeth,
And a blood-scenting snout —
All, like its muscular and sinuous body,
Evolved, genetically fashioned, for surprise attack.

Back home,
Free of white coats
And without laboratory scopes to peer,
We lean over the side of our old bay boat,
Resting on leather-cuffed oars,
Scouring the surface for bubbles,
The cut of a fin, the flick of a tail,
Or, just below, the momentary congestion
Of a looming shadow
That will break from bone's shallow
Into our morrow.

Dream Sequence

Symptoms weave in and out of my days.
They come to us the way the circus comes to town:
Top-hatted and high-stepping ringmasters bark out,
Solemn-stepping elephants follow,
Tail in trunk,
A single red-nosed clown
With bright shoes pointing left and right
Mocks the symmetry of the parade,
While sequined riders
With bouncing thighs and groins
Follow the mundane sawdust ring around
While a small band plays on.

We sneak a peek under the flapping canvas tent
Just as a tiger bounds into the large clanging cage.
A whip and a pistol shot put it
On its colorful high wood stool.
It sits up and growls,
Resentfully, obediently,
Pawing the air
Filled with jungle ghosts.
And we dream a world
Calling out for attention,
Suffer the sense
Of life's circus nonsense
And cancer's hushed presence.

The Mills Within

Worry sits on self's threshold,
And as best we can
We grind and round things pending
Into mute background.
We leave past to the rubble and stubble
Of fields forgotten.
We bridle augury and turn a stone-deaf ear
To prophecy.
Yet mills within and around
Grind, squeak, and growl.
The clandestine has wings,
A single fly buzzes,
A bat, a flying rabid rat,
Maliciously slices our barely lit room
Into a hundred segments,
And we coil inwardly
For one good final swat
To be delivered invisibly,
By the magic of particle physics,
The mercies of molecular chemistry.

No Oasis In *Osis*

There is no oasis
On malady's desert
And the etymological sands of *osis*,
(A Latin suffix for a hundred or so physiologic
And pathologic conditions and states).

Each disease —
Arteriosclerosis, cyanosis, cirrhosis, fibrosis —
Has ten to a hundred signs and symptoms,
Accounting for journeys of prognosis and hypnosis
Ever in search of diagnosis
On this wind-blown territory
Glimmering in mirages of therapy.

Please, let Lazarus put a drop of water on my parched lips
And throw a wet towel on my harrowed forehead.

Daily Augury

And so we tell time,
Calculate passing days and years
By counting the stars in the sky,
Diagnoses ten thousand times ten,
And symptoms like spring's abundant hatch of insects.
Who can count types of therapy, ways of augury?

So much occurs regularly and predictably,
A matter of rule and law,
Habit and practice.
However, then come surprises,
Accidents,
A call for compromises.

And we inch toward next with guesses and wishes,
Superstitions and intuitions.
Every possibility surmised and identified,
Each diagnosis apprised, advised,
Treatment tried.

In the corner
Of maybe, perhaps, hopefully,
We dance and sacrifice,
Give up puzzling next,
Trying to stay married
To flirting, embraceable now.

Riches

Love reaches beyond self.
Embracing, we are turned inside out,
Fly up beyond ourselves
On currents of grace not understood.

Ignorant of divine things given,
I know I am blessed,
By body, life, and hope
To be one with you.

And Then, Next

A few trust magic, charms, and spells,
The majority makes their crutches hunches.
They travel unknown space and time by guess and wish.

They cross streams
On slippery moss-covered rocks
Of omen and sign,
Under a portending moon
Seek a night's rest
On a harsh bed of broken dreams and forgotten prayers.

There are exceptional poet travelers,
Like Sun Wu,
Who served sixth-century regional King Helü of Wu,
But none know the coming season—
Not the diviners of the twelve animal signs of the Zodiac
Nor the practitioners foretelling magic.

None pass time's test,
Not the early scientists of subtle hypothesis,
Mathematicians of likelihood and probability,
Nor philosophers of gnosis.

Strategist and philosopher,
Honorifically known as Sun Tzu, "Master Sun,"
He offered decisive strategies for Wu's victories.
In distant smoke and rising dust,
He deciphered enemy numbers,
Espied the openings for a battle's beginning.
Yet remember accident and fortune fall out of the ken of all.

Be you general of a glorious land
Or a paltry corporal with torn and tarnished epaulettes
In a decommissioned regimental band,
One ordinary, unexpected day
That you will never divine,
You will die as never foreseen.

There is always *next*—
A crude and raw *then*,
An all-of-a-sudden divesting and redressing when.
Next belongs to no text,
It is without metrics.
Like a blood moon's rise,
It portends great surprise
As certain as sunrise.

Symptoms and Diagnoses

1

You ask how are symptoms and diagnoses,
All rolled into one,
Forever tumbling down the hill
Like Jack and Jill.

Simple enough, my friend.
If your mind has a poetic bent:
There is a coincidence of *here and nows*
And *then and theres*.

2

At every tick and tock
Of the clock,
The pendulum's long and short swing,
All that has been thought and said
Is thought, said, and wished again.

3

We are puppets
On taut and slack strings
Who go up and down,
Yo-yoed
On stories old
And yet to be told.

4

Even memory,
When all the hub-bub
And events and rigmarole are *kaput,*

Does not assure buoyancy.
Float our dead and us up —
However violently we tread,
It is oblivion's deep watery bottom
We dread.

5

Though mind is a fertile nest
Of copulating times,
Forgotten and imagined,
Conjured and augured,
There comes a hour
When all our young have fledged.

6

The old's bent and chalkless cue
Aims at tomorrow
With feeble projects and puny plans.
Life's circumference
Is staked out
By maladies and obituaries.

7

Mind smoothed
By ailing corpus and contested field
Has a dulled blade.
It divides
Diminished probabilities
By limited possibilities.

8

Mind's very wings,
Which once flew us far
In the directions of
Could be, might be, and should be,
Have lost their flap.

9

We, worn bees,
Cling to the sides of autumn hives,
Wherein honey is hope
That somehow grainy and seedy flowers,
Transformed,
Will fuel flights
Towards faith's
Ever-renewing maybe.

The Clandestine Body

A dozen organs,
Five major systems,
Cells, nerves, organs,
Brain, bones, teeth,
Marvelous machine,

Sources of hidden cancers,
An irregular heart beat,
A nervous tick,
A lifelong twitch,
A hundred wrongs and maladies,

Orifices,
Broken ducts,
Sealed and herniated tubes,
I shit too little
And I piss too much.

Symptoms manifest
And subtle,
A tremor, a shake,
Vertigo, a backache,
Ever felt but never pinpointed
Hide below my skin,
Within the body's tunnels and organs.

Like the earth's rumblings,
The truth belongs to guess,
To diagnosis,
The skill of a dozen crafts,
Ten probes,
Five shadowy films,

And twenty blood and lab tests.

And two hundred treatments
Lie ahead
In this rolled-and-tossed,
Crumpled bed.

The Way of the World

The world ever is in a spin,
Events rule.
Alive, we anticipate.

Hunches, guesses, suspicions,
They crowd and cling to consciousness:
Alert, aware, alarmed.

Senses perk and peak,
Eyes scan, scrutinize, squint.
The body gestures what the mind conjectures.

The field is never level:
Accident, possibility, coincidence ever
Apportion fortune.

Temperance tries
But cannot hold time,
Which rings its own eerie, echoing chime.

Epifania

On the day Fina died
Of an ectopic pregnancy,
A bird flew into her house.
Three months before,
A tea-leaf reader
Could find no fortune in the leaves of her empty teacup.
Two months before,
My mother found no lifeline
Crossing Fina's palm.

Fina, my dad's sister,
Had such a kind face and generous home,
And a good-natured pinochle-playing husband, Phil.
I was too young to mourn an aunt
I hardly knew.

Omens and Auguries

I do not have the world
In a locket.
And that same owl still stands on my balcony,
Hooting, softly, in moonlight:
Days and nights will soon be turned upside down.
In childhood's all-telling time,
A black bird flew into my pregnant aunt's house,
Announcing her death,
And I, seventy years later,
Still chase the fish that pouts the golden ring,
The bee, buzzing, humming,
That makes immortal honey.
In my pocket, I grip my father's jack knife —
Black, bone handle
With a freshly honed edge that cuts into the past,
Almost to the heart
Of love barely expressed.

Mourning a Red Pine

The limbless red-trunked pine,
Scorched by dry seasons,
Long and strong,
With only sparse yellow needles to shed,
Stands naked next
To a rising, spreading, grace-filled white pine.
A solitary red stick,
It stands helpless
As woodpeckers perfect
A hole-filled perimeter
In which bats dwell
And termites bore.
What is left of life
Rests in darkness within
As the pine rots in bright
Life-giving sunlight.

Time's Thread

Do not think of the death of all the animals,
Small and great,
The rotting of beloved trees,
Crumbling of mountains,
The volcanoes' birth of lush valleys.

Think simply, less cosmically,
Of the children dying in the womb
Of genetic defects
And those killed by their mother's choice.
Simply probe and riddle
Children dead at the suck of a dry nipple,
Mind whole generations lost in long migrations,
Cast on desert and ocean winds.

Christ died on the cross at thirty-three,
The same age my immigrant grandfather died
After an ordinary day's work in the factory.

Now seventy-seven —
A favorite age in my family for dying —
I cannot blind myself
To the legions of old,
Bent and bowed,
That melt around me,
Sure as the polar caps.

I, historian, cursed twice
To know endings aren't perfect
And nice,
Grow ever more aware
That the dead

Disappear on time's thread.
I can only hope
That Son and Spirit
Birth us anew,
Make us flesh-aware
Of our small but lasting share
Of telling form and love's lifting light.

At Port

I am past the age of I,
Ahab's avenging will.
I do not command the wheel,
Chart the course.
Rather I belong to port,
The retiring time of memory and me.
In this shortening season of vulnerable security
I ask what can God,
What will God, make of us,
Living and dead,
Now on earth and at sea,
And forever in Heaven.

Laws of Nature

Generous, merciless plentitude,
Ruthless plethora,
Spring, cruel in life's abundant flush,
Eggs washed away in a river's blind, wasteful rush,
A random quake,
Life's mortal cascade,
War's brutal parade,
Overturned cradles.

Life's bountiful inexactitudes
Deny certitude,
And I can only trudge earth's path
With the bent staff of Christian faith
And the hobble of hope.

A Poet's Work

Words,
Knots of prose,
Are the holding cordage
Of common days.

But I would make
Poetry and prayer
The gathering of the living and the dead,
The harvest of metaphor.

IV. PRAYERS

The Girl in the Rain

Her umbrella:
Fingers held over her head.
The more drops fall on her hair
The wider her smile,
The more she baptizes me
With joy.

Hummingbird

I know myself by the compass and quickness of my eye.
I followed the bird's frenetic flight, back and forth,
Through the clumsy metal furniture
Around the fountain and in and out of the trees
Of our pyramid-crowned atrium,
Until exhausted, when it came to rest
In the bottom corner
Of a large window by the door.

I knew myself by the touch of my fingers
That took and held the helpless jeweled thing
Cupped in my hands.

And I knew joy as I stepped outside
And opened my palms, the joy
Of returning this shimmering creature of flight and color
To the nectar of light and flower —
The rapture of giving back what is yours.

Birth

Birth welcomes us to soil and stars,
Our lives, a scoop of being in
God's Creation
And Son's Salvation.

Freed This Failing Flesh

Freed this failing flesh,
The cut and thorn of raspberry plant,
The bite of wild animal;
Relieved my own mean kind;
Delivered the remorseless human harvest of the day's news;
Spared this jumble of proud, contradictory thought
Divided between now and hereafter —
Is this then salvation?

No, there is no redemption in emptiness,
No wholeness in gnosis;
No fullness in knowledge,
Rebirth in elaborated truth.
There is salvation only in a promised land,
In a return to childhood,
The grace of being alive,
Mother's breast,
The feast of the family table,
The promise of again being with our dead,
Saturday afternoon's sin-free skip from church,
Having made a good confession,
And Sunday's Eucharist,
The single wafer of hope
That Jesus Christ
Is saving Lord and God.

Grace Abounds, Glory Redounds

Historian, I fill myself with stories and deeds,
Glory, virtue, and vice,
Misery, charity, and pity.
All things human
I strive to understand,
But I do not know the Ages of the
Creating Father,
Redeeming Son,
Enlightening Spirit.

In humbling ignorance,
Hopeful grace abounds,
God's glory redounds.

I Can't Write Salvation

I can remember family
And the past.
I can write them alive
By a careful and crafty repeating
Of word, genealogy, and story,
But I offer
Only books —
Not deliverance,
Redemption,
Salvation
From wilderness and sin.

I cannot think my way to a saving God
Who recalls the aborted eggs
Of spring's hatch
Against a river's torrential flush
And cascading death;
A God who returns flight to an unfledged dead hawk;
A God who has made a stark rack
Beyond hope and grace,
Just and adequate
For the terrorist race.

My reason gives no rest
Following the jagged ridge of worst and best,
Taking up the twists and turns of history,
The ways of cruel and good humanity.
I cannot reconcile beauty and mortality.
I cannot make rational toll
Of a being-swallowing sinkhole,
Of stars and sun now turned black and cold,

No longer lighting the way of wise, gift-bearing kings.

I am left
By dim day
And through the blur of years,
Padding,
Trudging,
Creeping a faithful circle
Around the Son's cross.
I wing up on an unexpected draft
Of beauty's epiphany,
Am kindled by love's impulse,
Live by the single
Unmerited and unfathomable hope
That salvation and redemption
Finally come,
That God's first and Son's second creations
Become truly one
In Trinity's everlasting kingdom.

No End

Transect an infinite line into an infinite number of points;
A three-dimensional compass rotates to other infinities.
Add and subtract, multiply and divide *ad infinitum.*
Space and time have no end.
And when I multiply an infinity
By the square of infinity,
I clash my hands
And pray this mind,
Gift of God
Now gone numbers wild,
Not shred a believing heart
And the hope we rise.

When

Then tell me,
If you can, of that time
When cleverness is not the game
And individuals who relinquish bids to fame
No longer suffer loss of name.
When prayer
And need of therapy
Silence ruminating philosophy
And when ideology's rush
Is made to go hush.
Then look for an oracle,
No, pray
With all the power of your stuttering heart
For a miracle.

These Bones

I read all surfaces,
Forms, shapes, faces, and palms of hands,
Spin compasses,
Try my graced hands on a ouija board.
Alone at night,
From a small porch
I read passing constellations,
Keep my eye peeled for the moon's waning.
In the morning I try a day's recipe,
Rub my scalp,
Knock on wood,
Bolt my door against a stray bird,
Put my shirt on inside out
For good luck.

My list of auguring grows long,
My magic tricks more,
But still my fate eludes me
Except I end scattered bones.

I can only dance and dance
To stir hope
That Ezekiel call me up
And that God breathe life
Into these dry bones
And that this sclerotic heart
See and touch
Stars.

So We Lament and Hope

I join Nonna Rosalia
And Sicilian women in black,
Scarecrows
In the back row
Of the carpeted parlor.
As they lament and tell
A lifetime of stories,
They form a cross of memory.
So they live by old hope
That remembering
Is to pray.

Weeping Willow

The weeping willow
Is nature's window.
Tall and upward reaching,
She is still draped in late summer's shawl
Of bright green
And long-hanging streamers.

This annual weave of leaf and branch
Hides a rotting trunk
And broken boughs,
Years of seasons' thrall.

Like any grandmother
Of thinning skin and loving heart,
She will shiver with winter's coming.
Yet rooted in earth, she is one with all,
The rising sun
And the slosh
Of deep water.

Easter

The ground is black and wet with spring,
Light and warmth blanket the earth,
Christ has risen,
Colors break forth,
My mind flies on forms toward the Creator,
I will every number to be random
And infinity beyond every number's square
Free of social scientists' awkward geometry
And politicians' raw and coarse touch
While love and hope quarrel
With the snags and tangles
Of our passing years.

The Light of the Day

For many-tongued reason
Things have abundant meanings
Made so by closely-woven nets
Of logic and definition,
By loose contrasts
And stone-certain and either/or juxtaposition.

Reason finds conviction
In seasons' laws of birth and death,
In irrevocable stages of life's evolution.

Then too stories beguile
With imagination's flight
While history's supple narrative
Laces lives and events together
With judgment and wisdom.

But only faith
Speaks to the wonders of birth, love, and death.
Its first and last counsel:
Take the light of the day
As God's gift to you
And trust
By soul and spirit
You are the form meant for forms
And the child intended
To love the creator of all forms.

A Night So Whole

A night so whole,
A moon so full,
A pine tree so tall and still,
But my eye leads to a rising slope
Of crystalline snow,
Graceful,
Luminous,
Of awakening promise.

V. NOW IS RIFE WITH NEXT

GREEK
dia
apart

GREEK
diagignöskein
distinguish,
discern

MODERN LATIN
diagnosis
late 17th century

GREEK
gignöskein
recognize,
know

1

One ordinary day thirty years ago, my doctor gave me, in the most matter of fact way, a double diagnosis: I had adult-onset diabetes and major heart blockage. No prognosis, other than the likelihood of eventual heart surgery, could be given without future tests.

Of a pensive disposition, I had since childhood given death a place in my mind. One of my earliest memories, as an only child with a bedroom of my own, was of falling asleep thinking one day I wouldn't be any more.

As a boy, I went to funerals and visited the cemetery. I had a favorite uncle die at a young age. I frequently heard my widowed Sicilian grandmother, ever dressed in black and with a votive candle on her bedroom dresser, call on God to take her. I was brought up Catholic, though attending public school, believing that this life was about dying and preparing for the next.

At university and later as a college history teacher, I was attracted to Spanish and Russian thought for its attention to subjectivity, tragedy, and death. I judged philosophies that did not acknowledge change and temporality superficial, and I would not subordinate to causes and explanation the reality of surprise and the power of events to define the human condition. My diagnosis was my 1789, 1914, 1917, or 1939 for Europe and 1941 for the United States. It was an earthquake whose aftershocks kept the ground under me trembling.

I was in mid-life. My career was flourishing with promotions, publications, and good colleagues, as much as it could at a new small four-year college locked since its beginnings in the late 1960s in endless struggles to survive, unionize, and stabilize itself in rural southwestern Minnesota. My wife, Cathy, had returned to full-time public health nursing. Our four children were out of or in college—on their way to independence. Our folks, Cathy's in northeastern Pennsylvania and mine in a suburb of Detroit, Michigan, seemed on a steady course. And then, the diagnosis came, scrambling expectations predicated on regular and repeating days ahead.

It jumbled the following month, now almost instantly crammed with a hospital stay and medical appointments and tests, which confirmed the heart troubles but offered only the prognosis of the need for eventual surgery. At some point, I would in all likelihood need a bypass. This diagnosis, which confirmed a pending mortal condition and offered as a prognosis what I took to be risky surgery, reframed my ways and days. It structured the next five years with a regime of exercise and diet. I prayed regularly—and found refuge from fears and anxieties in dwelling on the redeeming line "Thy Will be Done." However, I never entirely escaped the sense, to use a favorite metaphor of those times, that I was skating on black ice.

As I continued to teach, write, and help govern the history department, there were cracks in the black ice. My seventy-seven-year-old father died in an instant in his chair watching the University of Michigan play basketball grappling to win a national championship. He died of a heart attack, probably caused by underlying diabetes. We brought my seventy-seven-year-old mother to live with us in a nearby residence in Minnesota, so distant from the east side of Detroit, where she had lived seventy years. Her struggle, physical and mental, with my dad's bolt-sudden death and her own aging, furnished a large screen on which scenarios of how I might die, how my wife might age, how in a moment the known world might be cut in two—or yet painfully and perilously proceed. I was much humored by her abiding wit and her frequent diagnosis and prognosis of all life: "It's hell to get old!" If she got a laugh or needed to get her frustrations off her chest, she repeated it once or twice, prolonging the "l's" of "hell...l...l."

My prognosis was realized. Blockage in my main descending coronary artery reached over ninety percent. My cardiologist said he thought the time for surgery had arrived. I would live on at great risk of heart attack and stroke.

With a date set for surgery, I had a month to gather my thoughts and prayers. I had only to make a tentative farewell to my wife and children and tell a friend and a colleague or two at work. I resigned myself to surgery as a duty. I had come to a point where there was no choice.

I found some consolation in the idea that my condition would be met directly by surgery rather than diet and exercise. The matter of afterlife would be resolved for me. Perhaps, I could meet the dead family I loved. I could even meet and embrace Antonino, the grandfather who had died when my father was three and my grandmother Rosalia was again pregnant. I could see them in their youth together, dancing.

They had carried Sicilian fate to the new land of their dreams. They had been in America only long enough to move from a small town in the Pennsylvania Anthracite region to promising industrial Detroit. They were there for only a year or so when their first son, Joseph, was scalded to death by overturning Rosalia's scrub bucket. Then a few years later, in 1915, Antonino came home sick from work, and was dead by the next morning from appendicitis. Rosalia in a single blow was left alone with my father (also named Joseph) and expecting her next child, Epiphania (Fina). She had to find her way in this new world without a man. She would have to rely on the families of a nearby sister and brother and a few friends.

Perhaps in death I would be joining Antonino, along with my dad, and Rosalia and my mother's beloved parents, William and Frances, whose roots were in a small ethnic lumber and papermaking town in east central Wisconsin, along the Fox and Clinton rivers. Perhaps I would survive but have a stroke en route to having my heart repaired. Alive, but a crippled body and a mind and hand that couldn't control life with words and metaphors. So I went forward to medicine's cure, committing myself to its experts and its medicine with elemental anxiety, love of wife, and the most ancient mode of prayerfully asking and surrendering life into God's hands. Irritated by the stupidly superficial game show on television in the waiting room, I was rolled into surgery. On the way I imitated my mother and grandfather Bill's joking manner. I asked the young black orderly, as we rolled down the hall on my way to be under the knife and needle, if he would "like to trade places," playing on the very popular 1983 movie featuring Dan Aykroyd and Eddie Murphy, "Trading Places."

I lived, of course. I even wrote a book called *Bypass, A Memoir*, my way to absorb an experience and bring it as much as I could under the control of words and mind. The experience influenced my tendency to see life as belonging to contingency and happenings and even, I guess, pushed me to write an essay called "Then and Then Again," in which I divided as sharply as possible what happens as next from the explanation and even causality that would equate "next" with logical and sequential "therefore," "hence," and "thus." Diagnosis forever calls a patient to prognosis, which means entering all the realms of the mind (reason, memory, imagination, and will), entering into the wild. Such imprecise terms as "likelihood" and "improbability" haunt commonly trod paths.

Either starkly declared as part of a doctor's diagnosis and prognosis, or concluded or conjured by mind, death for me equally announces the arrival of an empty advent. It does not produce a child king or yet a new season of life. Rather, death, the great zero point of life, being, and consciousness, proclaims that everything we think, make, and love has an end. Death takes down the self, our very road through and out of this life and our bridge to imagining a future life. Death pulls down the curtain; it leaves an empty screen. And the mind flickers and dims in projections of the afterlife. Death exceeds medical description. It empties metaphors. It makes hollow and cosmetic our icons of paradise.

So thought and writing mentored me. They taught me to acknowledge death as absolute, reason void of understanding and hope. But they did not tame it. It stood at the center of nature, life, and history. It formed the indisputable core of relentless, remorseless change.

2

When Catherine, my wife of fifty years, was told three years ago that she had cancer, the door of our everyday life was breached again as it had been twenty-five years before when I was told I had diabetes and significant heart blockage. Impending and portending events overturned our days. Our minds were set racing to understand and treat, if possible, threatening conditions. We experienced suspenseful days and hours waiting for doctors' appointments and laboratory results.

As heart trouble threatens to strike like a bolt of lightening, so cancer, the crab, creeps clandestinely within. It brings to mind the old proverb: "Trouble arrives on horseback and departs on foot."

The very word "cancer," the crab, evokes the insidious, sly, sinister, and unpredictable. It evokes the black and ugly bottom and movement of things. It incites a riot of meanings with a plethora of forms and a multitude of dark possibilities. It conspires within our bodies—our bones and our lymph and even circulatory systems. Against it all flesh, human and animal, is vulnerable to exaggerated duplications.

Cancer placed Cathy, us, in the ring of continuing medical diagnosis. A nurse, long familiar with medical ways, she went forward without great anxiety and near fearlessly. Doctors and hospitals (and all their devices) were not alien to her.

As finally diagnosed at the Mayo Clinic in Rochester, Minnesota, she was found to have two distinct types of cancer—myeloma and lymphoma—both generated somehow in the marrow of her bones.

As her doctors established their diagnosis and refined their treatments over months, Cathy composed herself with patience, courage, and prayers. Proving herself the true daughter of Carpatho-Rusin mountain immigrants and coal miners, she resisted dwelling on speculations or bathing in pity about her own condition. She grasped that was to no avail. And she did all she could to escape being the object of idle conversation and speculation. Of course, she passed on all the information she had to our children: her genetic makeup might determine theirs.

I had a support role. I would drive to Mayo. There I would lend a second pair of ears to the doctor's advice and chase sandwich and soup for Cathy during her four-hour infusion.

Back at home I need only be a companion. We did simple things together. We went to younger grandchildren's games, enjoyed visits from and to our children, took frequent trips to the nearby library and YMCA, and watched a smattering of television, highlighted by the news and the entertainment of such programs as "Antiques Roadshow," "The Pickers," and "Downton Abbey." Aside from the excellent meals Cathy continued to prepare day in and day out, even on the days she herself didn't feel like eating, we shared an occasional bag of black licorice, read the *Wall Street Journal*, read our favorite literature, and took in, in print and on television, the 2016 Presidential primaries, which afforded cathartic relief.

Cathy's diagnosis, treatment, and prognosis took me back to times of my own heart trouble and my successful bypass operation, which came five years later. Her recently declared remission reminded me that at times hope is rewarded with good fortune and joy.

Our move from a home in a rural western Minnesota town to an apartment in a large high-rise senior residence in the western suburbs of the Twin Cities reinforced my thoughts about how we all, in body and mind, age and die, and hope differently. All these thoughts informed the poems found here and anticipated by my recent books, *Buoyancies: A Ballast Master's Log* and *My Three Sicilies: Stories, Poems, and Histories.*

3

To be modern is to live in a state of perpetual diagnosis. It can be to narrate our lives by medical events. Perennially we are creatures who project ahead, whose very survival as creatures depends on reading the threats and possibilities inherent in the present. We base our contemporary lives on our capacity to forecast, predict, calculate risk, and even insure on the basis of experience and probability. For us now is ever rife with next.

Diagnostics, the discipline of reading and concluding from evidence and symptom, is perhaps the first art of our modernity. We use it in design, experimentation, and repair. It forms medicine's dominant way of looking at our corporeal and mental conditions and gauging hopes for improvement.

Exacting quantitative measure and precise imaging extend the power of diagnostics by allowing us to isolate single cells and parts, and their functions and relations, while magnifying our sight and touch down to subatomic levels and into the most complex molecular and organic processes. The promise of diagnostics is projected as limitless. It even misleads some of us to think we can, or one day will be able to, diagnose the future of nature, society, and all individuals.

Diagnosis, the word and the activity, most often comes into our lives with medicine, our contemporary source of treatment, cure, and what by any measure of the past must be judged miracles. We meet it by surprise—we fall from a bike ... a friend's knee pops out of joint ... a favorite uncle, just married and at the start of family life, gets cancer and dies. Diagnosis, at least first diagnosis, comes swiftly and often departs begrudgingly, making us, our bodies and minds, an occasion for a gathering of cousin diagnoses and prognoses.

Medicine has its center at the nexus of being—the ever so real and ever so elusive point where body and spirit meet and surely are one and two; the point where mind and spirit cannot distinguish themselves.

Medicine checks us out in a hundred ways with hand and eye, chart and machine, laboratory tests and a host of devices to penetrate and probe our body and its systems. It guarantees our health to go to school, to play, to join the army, to travel. It listens to our symptoms and wants; discerns our sicknesses and health; and responds with therapy, cures, and prognosis.

Medicine's dominion has grown vastly in the last hundred and fifty years. It is part of an immense movement toward a great industry of science and research, doctors and hospitals, drugs and cures. It speaks in the privacy of any office or through an official pronouncement. Its subject can be the individual in a condition at a moment or, at the other extreme, the epidemiological diagnosis of society's wellness in the face of a rapidly spreading mysterious disease or the potential course of a malady rooted in a weather pattern, deteriorating water condition, sanitation facilities, or spreading dietary habits.

Increasingly over the last century and a half in the United States and throughout much of the world, modern medicine has displaced traditional medicine and its limited capacity to diagnose and treat with cosmology, magic, superstitions, augury, and traditional religious practices and beliefs. Medicine increasingly trumps guessing. As it follows and in some cases precedes and stimulates theoretical science and advancement in measurement, materials, and technology, medicine is heralded for its success and becomes by popular opinion and law the established voice of authority in matters of life and death.

Medicine wears the humane face of progress. It gives science, chemistry, and technology a humanistic agenda. Its systematic and broad concern for all justifies research, invention, manufacture, and spending. Accounting for increased well-being and longevity for the majority, medicine is voted for by the majority with their feet and by society in augmenting its budget for medical treatment.

In the spirit of early medicine and the medieval hospital, today's doctors, clinics, and emergency wards stand open to taking on an individual's suffering, maladies, disease, and injuries. By law and regulation, sanitation, safety, and public health agencies are organized and funded to diagnose the ongoing conditions and specific vulnerability of whole groups, industries, and populations.

And with its astronomically expanded ability to measure and utilize atoms, synthetize and manipulate molecules, select, foster, and kill cells, and intervene in human genetics and reproduction, contemporary medicine diagnoses and cures as it and nothing else ever did before. Its descriptions and prescriptions recognize and treat the unwanted and realize new dreams. Its removal of pain and broad-front war against mortality itself command universal attention and evoke respect and reverence for it and its vast array of general and ever-specialized workers — doctors, dentists, surgeons, nurses, teachers, technicians, epidemiologists, researchers, and aides of every sort. While the living flock in for the diagnoses and prognoses of medicine, the priest and the religious are left tending the dead and the afterlife with "good counsel," grace, and miracles.

Twenty-three years after a quadruple bypass operation, I owe my own life to medicine. And it now holds the hand of my wife as we walk towards cancer's cure or stalemate. In truth, I cannot inventory the countless ways in which medicine has served the world's and my well-being and longevity. It has mollified pain, given the suffering hope, and driven remorseless and adventitious death from the door. It has issued warnings, taught prevention, diagnosed and cured maladies, and allowed us to shape and manipulate our own bodies for the sake of our reproduction, health, work, and creativity.

But medicine has not compassed my mind when I think of the course of time, the temporality of all things, including peoples and cultures, and my own death.

As a young man I was drawn to history not as a matter of biography, people, or a set of events, but as a way to understand philosophy and religion. At the center of this interest stood the commanding question of how we make sense out of time — with myth and ritual, philosophy and argument, religion, symbols, and belief. This focused my fervor on the study of primitive mentalities, the Greeks and pre-philosophy, and medieval thought. My return to my youthful Catholicism, lost and then found in a matter of two emotional years, gave me back the central belief that God transcendental and Christ incarnate assure hope of redemption and lasting love.

At twenty, a first-semester junior at the University of Michigan, I read in the works of Mircea Eliade, Arthur Maurice Hocart, and others the idea that traditional peoples used both rituals and myths to speak of the beginnings of a time and to assure its renewal. I immediately embraced this as true. Here was the freeing notion that myth as metaphor and poetry furnished the first language of talking about time and our place in it. Metaphors, the wings of poetry, place us in being. Myths testify to the wondrous glory of being yet the insurmountable tragedy of living.

Myths recognize realities and order time. Time changes life and things with accident, development, happening, and event. Time turns the kaleidoscope of actions and thought, conditions, and circumstances. In prehistory and history we find the sacramental grounds of myth and ritual, beliefs, ideas and worldviews about our genesis, fates and fortunes, and ends. In a narrative woven into the revelation of a Providential God we find a faith language for talking about our mortality.

I quickly embraced the idea that our commanding myth was to reenact and call up "a spring of springs," that is, an annual renewal, a restoration, renovation, and renaissance, nothing less than the rebirth of life itself. I took the central goal of primitive and traditional myth to be the end of winter and the rebirth of spring and creation.

This belief molded and defined by faith called for and acclaimed a transcendental rescue; not just an intellectual point beyond all other points but a spring of rebirth that would restore and make us whole in good will, hope, and glimmering joy. No thing, no age, no single saving idea, however emotionally and aesthetically elaborated, offered me such a rescue from time, and death. As much as the world offered love, form, beauty, and knowledge, it did not undo aging, chaos, disaster, catastrophe, and tragedy or afford hope against the test of events.

In Christianity I found the point where myth and history meld. As C. S. Lewis put it in *Surprised by Joy* (1955):

> The heart of Christianity is a myth which is also a fact . . . We pass from a Balder (an old Norse God) or an Osiris, dying nobody knows where or when, to a historical Person . . . under Pontius Pilate. By becoming fact it does not cease to be miracle. To be truly Christian we must both assent to the historical fact and also receive the myth (fact though it has become) with the same imaginative embrace which we accord to all truths.

My study of history itself has been a long journey. From an appreciation of all people's reliance on myths to construct meaning, I moved unconsciously to folklore and ethnography to an increasing appreciation of my own family background as rural, peasant, and working class and of the popular and folk cultures by which they gave sense and purpose to life.

I have concluded that all cultures and individuals continually think, feel, and diagnose their place in time. The present is full of the revealing past, dawning future, and imminent next. With wellness and fulfillment of body and mind the axis of attention and the hub of our energies, we are chock-full of hunches, forethoughts, and guesses. Traditional medicine, with its roots in early cultures and civilization, fed on touch and prayers, augury, superstition, numerology, and sharp scalpels and hooks to enter every orifice and cranny of the body. In the traditional world—which remains in measure mine—clues, guesses, suspicions, symptoms, as well as wishes, hopes, and prayers, serve as primary means to navigate the world. As much as I believe that humans have intelligence, can distinguish good and bad ideas, discern evidence of great variety, make keen judgments, and even arrive at wisdom and sturdy character, I still believe we are led to prayer and faith in God's grace.

I never lent my heart to faith in progress insofar as it promises a peaceful and harmonious, a pain- and suffering-free future. I was never tempted to believe that humans could or should take control of their own destinies. During the Vietnam War I concluded that states constricted lives and that nations, however enlightened, could never reduce the world to a matter of problems and solutions. I discounted the application of the felicific calculus of pleasure and pain to individuals and whole societies.

Increasingly, I believed that the next of happenings is not to be confused with the next of certain reasoned consequence: the logic of therefore, hence, thus, and so. Dissenting from the proposition that causality as a system is applicable to specific cases and predictive of the future, on the personal front, I with aging assented more and more to Herodotus and his judgment on attaining human happiness based on the fate of King Croesus: "Count no man as happy until he is dead."

On the historical front, I agreed with Henry Adams. We never learn much. Ignorance prevails when it comes to the future. Our control over nature, as typified by the dynamo and the imagined possibility of splitting the atom, accelerates astronomically; but nevertheless change escapes understanding. Events ever outrun intelligence.

These ideas set me against the optimistic claims of much of the secular world with its utopian promises. Enlightenment beliefs in progress through knowledge and science, so embodied in American and Western politics and economics, seemed not only false but deadly when joined to thorough-going rationalizing and the unbounded, all-powerful state. Utopias based on all-inclusive ideologies, endless technology, and political efficiency birth totalitarianism.

Historian that I am, I assume that time baffles. Surely the past is not fully read, the present understood, or the future written by our design. For me, accordingly, diagnosis and prognosis, however beneficially advanced, are bounded by guess and surprise. No matter our triumphs over outer space and the inner worlds of molecule, atom, and gene, man does not fully command his own body and mind or fully stand beyond nature, life, and time. Limits prevail; accidents intercede; and events propel our kind collectively beyond assured command, as Cathy and I, but two of billions of humans, prayerfully go on, traveling weekly in hope of a treatment that cures and sustains.

5

So contemporary medicine does not coincide with our traditional mode of meeting, "hashing through," to use a favorite phrase of Cathy's, the next in now. Undoubtedly, older superstitions and auguries about the weather, coming events, and portentous fates have failed on many counts in the face of modern predictions and forecasts based on probability and pinpoint analysis in the case of coming weather and select natural occurrences. Contemporary demography and polling techniques for voting and advertisements, with all their gaps (especially about intensity and surges of passions) and faulty generalizations based on select places, have largely superseded hunches and guesses born of intuitions, standing wisdom, and past experience.

Contemporary diagnostics have triumphed over traditional predictions in three vast areas. First, new machines, materials, and distribution of goods and ideas have defined society and culture. Second, insurance has wagered vast sums of money on the likelihood of individual and collective death and accident—on land, sea, and air—and for two centuries greatly won. Third, as argued in this essay, contemporary medicine has succeeded in singularly inventorying, preventing, and even curing human (and animal) maladies and diseases. It has, I surmise, superseded, even diminished, prayers for miraculous intervention. Women, like my older Sicilian relatives, have been taken, so to speak, out of their black mourning dress; fewer votive candles are lit in Catholic churches; and, to make my general point, lamentations, keening, and calls for mercy have been sequestered in old souls, while trips to medical clinics, counselors, and insurance agencies conduct our transactions with the future.

Traditional approaches to time — what I call the poetics of time — were richly expressed in rituals, magic, proverbs, myths, metaphors, stories, and literature. They defined the landscape with totems, sacred outlooks and grottos, restorative springs, and augured temples; they populated water and air with invisible spirits; and gods took up earthly and heavenly matters of strange occurrences, unexpected fortunes, and the appearance of benign kings, evil princes and witches, and representatives from all kingdoms and quarters of being.

Today medicine, thanks to transport and communications, meets the injured, the infected, the sick and dying where they are (at home, on battlefields, along highways, and on city streets) and transports them to clinic or hospital; or it delivers treatments and prescriptions to them on the spot. Science continually equips medicine with new pharmaceuticals and diagnostic techniques. It offers with treatments, protocols, and medicines more precise and hopeful prognoses. It designs tests and makes machines that identify and locate invisible atomic particles and molecules as well as read and alter the functions of genes and cells. Diagnosis, prognosis, and treatment form separate kingdoms of treatment; they create institutions and unleash revolutions of hope. With a man on the moon and organ transplants as proof of their validity, scientific advances account for gigantic projects of unprecedented hopes. Medicine, the most personal face of science, offers the best description of the human condition and offers, if not immortality, cure and relief for us infected, sick, and vulnerable earthly beings.

Surely, medicine remains the best immediate hope for Cathy and me. Yet, contemporary society and medicine do not speak to or for the dead or lasting justice, eventual reconciliation, and love fulfilled. So, because of and for the sake of hope, we stand firm in the grace of God's creation and Christ's salvation.

124

* * *

For man, all that is portends something next—many things
next. What is warns and invites, with endless synonyms and
antonyms. There is ever a next looming, hidden, in now: some-
thing fresh to be thought in yesterday, today, and tomorrow.
Diagnostics belong to—make—the mind. They read the next in
now. There forever is myth and poetry in then, now, tomorrow,
and hereafter. Metaphors, reaching from this to that, here to
there, are ever called into service of knowing, predicting, and
hoping. So we pray ever travelling between two worlds as I
write in this concluding poem titled "Conversion to Medicine
Tells."

I forsook enemas and purges,
No longer offered my body
To obsidian knives,
Penetrating brass hooks,
And boring trepanning drills.
I withdrew body and mind
From old medicine's diagnosis and cures.

Without trust in omens and auguries
Or means for the long saving pilgrimage,
I lit precariously flickering candles
And entered a religious order,
Praying to be spared pain now
And ever after.

Then one day, I became contemporary.
I surrendered myself body and soul
To advancing medicine.
I let its cuff squeeze my arm,
Its scope listen at my chest,
Its needles prick, and its tests
Measure my blood and biopsy my flesh.

Its instruments entered every organ and orifice,
Crooked and straight,
My brain was probed.
With each invasion I surrendered myself
To its tests and calculations.
Quartered on graphs and charts,
Taken into custody,
Held for mounting scrutiny
And experimental therapy,
I am opened to all penetrating pharmacy.

Biology and chemistry,
Physics too,
Machines for molecular and subatomic probes,
Medicine knows and swallows me whole.
I belong to its descriptions
And regimes of prescriptions.

My gratitude
Is great
For what medicine spares me and mine,
Giving hope of long earthly health.
It gave me a saving bypass twenty-five years ago;
And pills, morning and evening,
Permit me to walk the high wire
Over heart attacks
And contain diabetes' beachheads.
And today, spur to these reflections,
Medicine treats my wife for a complex marriage of two cancers
Bone deep in her.

Yet medicine doesn't replace
The bread and wine held high,
Or hold me on the shore of diagnosis and prognosis
When my mind sets sail on the *Pequod*
With commonsensical Ishmael and devout Starbuck,
Tattooed Queequeg and mad Ahab
In search of what the sea counsels.

VIA FOLIOS

A refereed book series dedicated to the culture of Italians and Italian Americans.

DENNIS BARONE. *Second Thoughts*. Vol 121. Poetry. $10
OLIVIA K. CERRONE. *The Hunger Saint*. Vol 120. Novella. $12
GARIBLADI M. LAPOLLA. *Miss Rollins in Love*. Vol 119. Novel. $24
JOSEPH TUSIANI. *A Clarion Call*. Vol 118. Poetry. $16
JOSEPH A. AMATO. *My Three Sicilies*. Vol 117. Poetry & Prose. $17
MARGHERITA COSTA. *Voice of a Virtuosa and Coutesan*. Vol 116. Poetry. $24
NICOLE SANTALUCIA. *Because I Did Not Die*. Vol 115. Poetry. $12
MARK CIABATTARI. *Preludes to History*. Vol 114. Poetry. $12
HELEN BAROLINI. *Visits*. Vol 113. Novel. $22
ERNESTO LIVORNI. *The Fathers' America*. Vol 112. Poetry. $14
MARIO B. MIGNONE. *The Story of My People*. Vol 111. Non-fiction. $17
GEORGE GUIDA. *The Sleeping Gulf*. Vol 110. Poetry. $14
JOEY NICOLETTI. *Reverse Graffiti*. Vol 109. Poetry. $14
GIOSE RIMANELLI. *Il mestiere del furbo*. Vol 108. Criticism. $20
LEWIS TURCO. *The Hero Enkido*. Vol 107. Poetry. $14
AL TACCONELLI. *Perhaps Fly*. Vol 106. Poetry. $14
RACHEL GUIDO DEVRIES. *A Woman Unknown in Her Bones*. Vol 105. Poetry. $11
BERNARD BRUNO. *A Tear and a Tear in My Heart*. Vol 104. Non-fiction. $20
FELIX STEFANILE. *Songs of the Sparrow*. Vol 103. Poetry. $30
FRANK POLIZZI. *A New Life with Bianca*. Vol 102. Poetry. $10
GIL FAGIANI. *Stone Walls*. Vol 101. Poetry. $14
LOUISE DESALVO. *Casting Off*. Vol 100. Fiction. $22
MARY JO BONA. *I Stop Waiting for You*. Vol 99. Poetry. $12
RACHEL GUIDO DEVRIES. *Stati zitt, Josie*. Vol 98. Children's Literature. $8
GRACE CAVALIERI. *The Mandate of Heaven*. Vol 97. Poetry. $14
MARISA FRASCA. *Via incanto*. Vol 96. Poetry. $12
DOUGLAS GLADSTONE. *Carving a Niche for Himself*. Vol 95. History. $12
MARIA TERRONE. *Eye to Eye*. Vol 94. Poetry. $14
CONSTANCE SANCETTA. *Here in Cerchio*. Vol 93. Local History. $15
MARIA MAZZIOTTI GILLAN. *Ancestors' Song*. Vol 92. Poetry. $14
MICHAEL PARENTI. *Waiting for Yesterday: Pages from a Street Kid's Life*. Vol 90. Memoir. $15
ANNIE LANZILOTTO. *Schistsong*. Vol 89. Poetry. $15
EMANUEL DI PASQUALE. *Love Lines*. Vol 88. Poetry. $10
CAROSONE & LOGIUDICE. *Our Naked Lives*. Vol 87. Essays. $15

RACHEL GUIDO DE VRIES. *Teeny Tiny Tino's Fishing Story*. Vol 47. Children's Literature. $6

EMANUEL DI PASQUALE. *Writing Anew*. Vol 46. Poetry. $15

MARIA FAMÀ. *Looking For Cover*. Vol 45. Poetry. $12

ANTHONY VALERIO. *Toni Cade Bambara's One Sicilian Night*. Vol 44. Poetry. $10

EMANUEL CARNEVALI. *Furnished Rooms*. Vol 43. Poetry. $14

BRENT ADKINS. et al., Ed. *Shifting Borders. Negotiating Places*. Vol 42. Conference. $18

GEORGE GUIDA. *Low Italian*. Vol 41. Poetry. $11

GARDAPHÈ, GIORDANO, TAMBURRI. *Introducing Italian Americana*. Vol 40. Italian/American Studies. $10

DANIELA GIOSEFFI. *Blood Autumn/Autunno di sangue*. Vol 39. Poetry. $15/$25

FRED MISURELLA. *Lies to Live By*. Vol 38. Stories. $15

STEVEN BELLUSCIO. *Constructing a Bibliography*. Vol 37. Italian Americana. $15

ANTHONY JULIAN TAMBURRI, Ed. *Italian Cultural Studies 2002*. Vol 36. Essays. $18

BEA TUSIANI. *con amore*. Vol 35. Memoir. $19

FLAVIA BRIZIO-SKOV, Ed. *Reconstructing Societies in the Aftermath of War*. Vol 34. History. $30

TAMBURRI. et al., Eds. *Italian Cultural Studies 2001*. Vol 33. Essays. $18

ELIZABETH G. MESSINA, Ed. *In Our Own Voices*. Vol 32. Italian/American Studies. $25

STANISLAO G. PUGLIESE. *Desperate Inscriptions*. Vol 31. History. $12

HOSTERT & TAMBURRI, Eds. *Screening Ethnicity*. Vol 30. Italian/American Culture. $25

G. PARATI & B. LAWTON, Eds. *Italian Cultural Studies*. Vol 29. Essays. $18

HELEN BAROLINI. *More Italian Hours*. Vol 28. Fiction. $16

FRANCO NASI, Ed. *Intorno alla Via Emilia*. Vol 27. Culture. $16

ARTHUR L. CLEMENTS. *The Book of Madness & Love*. Vol 26. Poetry. $10

JOHN CASEY, et al. *Imagining Humanity*. Vol 25. Interdisciplinary Studies. $18

ROBERT LIMA. *Sardinia/Sardegna*. Vol 24. Poetry. $10

DANIELA GIOSEFFI. *Going On*. Vol 23. Poetry. $10

ROSS TALARICO. *The Journey Home*. Vol 22. Poetry. $12

EMANUEL DI PASQUALE. *The Silver Lake Love Poems*. Vol 21. Poetry. $7

JOSEPH TUSIANI. *Ethnicity*. Vol 20. Poetry. $12

JENNIFER LAGIER. *Second Class Citizen*. Vol 19. Poetry. $8

FELIX STEFANILE. *The Country of Absence*. Vol 18. Poetry. $9

PHILIP CANNISTRARO. *Blackshirts*. Vol 17. History. $12

LUIGI RUSTICHELLI, Ed. *Seminario sul racconto*. Vol 16. Narrative. $10

LEWIS TURCO. *Shaking the Family Tree*. Vol 15. Memoirs. $9

LUIGI RUSTICHELLI, Ed. *Seminario sulla drammaturgia*. Vol 14. Theater/Essays. $10

CPSIA information can be obtained
at www.ICGtesting.com
Printed in the USA
FFOW02n0927170718
47412957-50606FF